Florence Montgomery

A very simple story, being a chronicle of the thoughts and feelings

of a child

Florence Montgomery

A very simple story, being a chronicle of the thoughts and feelings of a child

ISBN/EAN: 9783743355354

Manufactured in Europe, USA, Canada, Australia, Japa

Cover: Foto ©Suzi / pixelio.de

Manufactured and distributed by brebook publishing software
(www.brebook.com)

Florence Montgomery

A very simple story, being a chronicle of the thoughts and feelings

of a child

"HOW ABSORBING IS THE INTEREST OF SEEING NURSE DRESS!"

A VERY SIMPLE STORY;

BEING A

CHRONICLE OF THE THOUGHTS AND FEELINGS OF A CHILD.

ILLUSTRATED BY

THE MARCHIONESS OF QUEENSBERRY
AND M. R.

WRITTEN AND ILLUSTRATED EXPRESSLY FOR THE BENEFIT OF THE
FUNDS OF

A VILLAGE INDUSTRIAL EXHIBITION.

SLEAFORD,
PRINTED BY W. FAWCETT, MARKET-PLACE.
1867.

A VERY SIMPLE STORY.

—✦—

CHAPTER I.

VERY early this morning did the golden head raise itself from its white pillows, and watch the line of light that crept through the chinks of the closed shutters.

"Would it ever, ever be time to get up?"

"Could not the daylight hurry a *little* bit on this morning, of all mornings in the year; or, was it possible that the sun did not know that it is Maye's birthday?"

This was a new idea, and the golden head lay very still, while the busy brain revolved the question.

"God knew: yes, Maye was very sure God knew, for had not mother told her He knew *everything*. Well! God was in the sky, and the sun was in the sky. Might not God just have whispered it to the sun?" ·

"Maye will ask mother. *She* will be sure to know."

But that last ray of sunlight streams on nurse's face, and she stirs and rises.

Maye lies very still, watching her.

How absorbing is the interest of seeing nurse dress! How

A

neatly one thing goes on the top of the other, and how easily and quickly they are all put on. How well Maye knows the inch and a half of hair which nurse combs with such care; and then, with a skilful twist of her arm, transforms into a hard round knot, which is supported at the back of her head by one hair pin. Maye has often wondered what would happen if nurse lost that one hair pin! It is so peculiar, so bent, and all the black rubbed off by constant use, so that Maye is quite sure there is no other like it, in the world. Mother's hair pins are *quite* different, they are straight, and black, and shiny.

Now comes the crackling cotton gown and the white apron; the knot is hidden by the white cap; and—nurse is ready!

It has come at last, the moment so longed for, and Maye springs out of bed, and goes through the washing and dressing with tolerable composure, considering her age and circumstances.

Then she trots down the passage, through the swing door, on to the corridor that leads to mother's room, and knocks gently at the door.

Maye is full of importance now, for she has come to "say my prayers."

Golden haired child! standing there in the bright morning sunlight; does no sad presentiment of the dark days that are coming, steal over you? No thought of the time, when in cold and darkness you shall stand at that same door, and knock; but there shall be no answer for ever? .... Thank God! no. The future is mercifully hidden from us.

"JUST WHAT MAVE GUESSED : MOTHER IS "SAVING HER PRAYERS."

As no one answers, Maye opens the door, and peeps in. Just what Maye guessed! Mother is " saying her prayers."

There she kneels, Maye's beautiful young mother! She has golden hair, like the child's; and the sunbeams, streaming through the window, play on the rippling tresses of her bowed head. as if they loved to rest on anything so bright and fair. Maye stands very still, watching her.

" I wonder if mother will soon have done," she thinks to herself, " mother's prayers are very long: they are *so* much longer than mine *now*, but some day I will say very very long ones, perhaps as long as father's ! I *do* wonder why he always says his in the dining-room. They must be very grand ones, for all the servants go in to hear him : no one but mother comes to hear me ! I wonder"................

But the train of thought and wonder is interrupted, for the young mother has risen from her knees, and is holding out her hands. The golden hair of the mother, and the golden hair of the child, blend and become one for an instant as a fond kiss is imprinted on the little upturned face.

" So it is your birthday, my darling," says the soft loving voice, " God bless you, my child, and preserve you to me for many many years."

And then, with folded hands, Maye kneels by her mother's side, and repeats her baby prayer.

This ceremony over, the long-restrained chatter bursts forth, and trotting about the room, she examines every little corner, and asks the use of every ornament on the dressing table ;

which examinations have been made, and which questions
have been put, daily, ever since Maye was able to speak.

Willingly would she linger on in "mother's room" that
realization of all that is happy and delightful to these tiny
creatures, in whom mother-love is almost a religion ; but the
nursery breakfast is waiting, and she must hurry back.

So, with as many farewells and kisses as if a trackless jour-
ney lay before her, the child at length runs off.

She listens with her usual interest to all that nurse, and
Letty, the nursery-maid, have to say during that meal.

"They do say such curious things sometimes that she
cannot understand them, and she has often resolved to ask her
mother what it all means ; but generally by the time she gets
downstairs, she can hardly remember anything they said."

"Perhaps nurse and Letty would be just as pleased she
would not."

Breakfast over, Maye trots down the wide oak staircase, and
her little feet go pitter-patter along the gallery, till she comes
to the dining-room.

Here she meets all the servants coming from "hearing
Father his prayers," and she looks at them with a certain kind
of awe, as at privileged beings, admitted to mysterious doings
in which she has no share.

"For," she reflects to herself with a sigh, "they must all
know that Mother says I am "too young to come to Father's
prayers !"

This great degradation does not seem to affect the servants

with any very intense contempt for the tiny creature who stands gazing at them with her great blue eyes, as they file out into the gallery; for each has a word or a smile for her as they pass; and the old butler throws open the door, and she runs into the breakfast-room. Mother and Father are standing by the table, reading a letter together, and they are both laughing very much.

Maye's father is very tall, and has dark hair. Many people think him grave and stern, but Maye's mother can always make him laugh, and Maye herself is not at all afraid of him.

He comes quickly forward when he catches sight of his little daughter, and he lifts her up in his arms, and covers her with kisses till she is nearly smothered; and mother comes to the rescue, and says she shall be very jealous.

Father turns to her, and says " Jealous of me, or of Maye ?" And mother laughs her pretty soft laugh and says " Both." Upon which he smiles, and gives one lingering kiss on her forehead.

What it all means, Maye does not quite know, but she does not understand public attention being withdrawn from herself, so she puts her golden head in between them, and then they both kiss her at once.

Now the hissing urn is brought in, and mother makes the tea, while father reads the newspaper, and Maye stands very quiet and good by the table, with her chin resting thereon, and a pair of big blue eyes fixed on a paper parcel which is lying close by.

"Look, not touch," she whispers to herself two or three times to quell the burning desire her little fingers have to undo the parcel, which she is quite *sure* must be her birthday present! but not feeling very certain of her own powers of resistance, she puts her hands behind her and squeezes them tight together.

She is soon rewarded, for she catches mother's eye and mother is smiling, and father has put down the newspaper, and he is smiling too; and soon, sitting on father's knee, her trembling fingers wrestle with the wrappings, and a deep-drawn sigh "Oh dear me" escapes from the little rounded mouth at the sight of a wax doll.

Retiring to the floor with her new treasure, Maye is soon deep in a game, and it is so absorbing that she is quite startled when she hears her mother say "Now my darling must go out for her walk."

How hard it seems, just as dolly is so very interesting!

But when mother says a thing, though she says it very gently, Maye knows it has to be done; and so she carries dolly off upstairs, and they are soon both dressed and in the garden.

Dolly is taken to Maye's own little garden to see how the flowers are coming up, and then has a turn on the terrace, and is finally seated in the arbour.

Now this is all very amusing for Maye, but nurse wearies of it. "Miss Maye," says she "we will walk down the park to the lodge; it will be better than dawdling about the garden."

It is very odd, this, about nurse! She *always* likes to walk down the park to the lodge, and odder still, she always walks at the very edge of the park, where a paling divides it from the high road.

Somehow too, she generally finds friends passing along the high road.

Sure enough, as they go along, a voice on the other side of the hedge, says, " Good day to you Mrs. Nurse," and nurse stops and talks for some time.

Presently Maye hears the voice say " There's a deal of sickness in the village, and I can't rightly make out what it is; some kind of a fever, I reckon, but it do seem a quick spreading one, sure-*ly*, for there's two down with it on t'other side of the mill, and Widow Barton's little lad was took last night."

" What does he say ?" cries Maye, running up, " is anything the matter with Johnnie Barton ?"

" Hush " she hears nurse say to the man, " don't say a word before the child ; Mrs. Forrester is so afraid of infection for her, and Miss Maye would be sure to tell her, I wouldn't for the world my mistress should know there is a fever in the village. Run away, dear," she added, turning to Maye, " I am busy talking.

The child retreated a few steps, but she had heard enough to rouse her curiosity, and she listened with all her might.

But the conversation was now carried on in such low tones, that she heard nothing further, till the man moved on saying, " Well goodbye, Mrs. Nurse, and I'm glad to have met you."

Glad ! If any one could have told them what were to be

the results of that chance meeting! For some reason, nurse changed her mind about going to the village, and turned sharply off into the most secluded parts of the park.

Maye knew Widow Barton's little boy; he was her mother's favorite little pupil at the Sunday school, and had once or twice been up to the Hall to play with her; so she tried to find out what was the matter with him.

"Nurse" said she "is Johnnie ill?"

But nurse said hastily "Don't be tiresome, child, and, Miss Maye" she added, "Don't be bothering your mother about little Johnnie."

Now Maye was a wise child and made no rash promises, but she shrugged her shoulders rather pettishly, and fell into a train of thought.

"Mother is never bothered," she inwardly reflected, and never says "don't be tiresome child. I shall just tell her all about it directly I get home. I daresay she can give poor Johnnie some medicine to make him quite well again." Nurse did not talk any more during the walk and Maye wondered what made her so grave and silent.

"Mother," said little Maye at luncheon that day, "Johnnie Barton is ill."

"Ill!" said Mrs. Forrester, "little Johnnie Barton! how do you know Maye?"

But here Maye's memory rather failed her, and she answered vaguely that some one on the other side of the park palings had said so.

"Not very clear," said Mrs. Forrester laughing; then to her husband "I think, Gervase, I will go and see what is the matter with him. Poor Mrs. Barton is always at her wits' end if anything ails the boy, and knows no more than a baby what to do. I might drive down in the pony carriage after luncheon, and if you can't come with me, I daresay I could get a small companion, in consideration of its being her birthday."

"I am afraid" answered he "that I must ride over to those outlying farms to meet the bailiff, otherwise I should have liked to have driven you both; but I will not be quite cut out of these birthday doings," he added, turning with a smile to his little daughter, "for that would not be fair, Maye, would it? So, as you will be home earlier than me, you might bring mother across the fields, after your drive, to meet me. Unless it would tire you, Mabel?" he questioned, looking at his wife with a peculiar expression she well knew, and which told her, as plain as words could speak, that he only put the question that he might evoke the pretty soft laugh his ear delighted in, and see his answer in the bright look that broke all over her beautiful face.

The bell was rung, the orders given, and Maye was sent up to the nursery to dress.

"Nurse," says the important little voice "please put on my things quick. I am going to drive with mother to see............

But somehow Maye thinks she will not tell nurse where mother and she are going.

She does not know why, but she has a vague feeling, connected with the morning's walk, that nurse does not like poor Johnnie, and might perhaps put some objection in the way.

So nurse dresses her in happy ignorance, and then little Maye runs down to meet mother in the hall.

The pony carriage is at the door, and old John lifts her in.

Father and mother are talking together in the doorway, and laughing.

How pretty Mother looks to-day! Maye wonders she had not noticed it before.

Her face is lighted up as she talks to father, and her eyes are dancing and sparkling with happiness.

Father is leaning against the hall door, looking down upon her with his usual grave smile. He is just going to start for his ride, and has on his boots and spurs, and a riding whip in his hand, with which he is playing with the buttons of mother's coat.

Aye! look, little Maye! gaze, and gaze again on that sweet picture of summer sunshine and joy; for already the dark clouds are looming and gathering in the distance.

Could no kind angel step in, and warn them all from the doom to which they are hastening? But already it is too late: already is the first step taken from the sunshine into the shade; and the shadow shall deepen for ever and ever, till all is wrapped in gloom!

For, with a gay laugh and a parting wave of the hand to her husband, Mabel Forrester steps into the pony carriage and drives quickly away from the door.

Merrily chatters little Maye on the way to the village.

She has something to say of every bird that flies past, and of every flower in the hedge.

There is so much to ask this beautiful May-day; for the pretty spring flowers are everywhere bursting into life, the air is full of the songs of a thousand birds, the young lambs sport in every field they pass, and the blossoms on the trees look bright in the gay sunshine.

And then, Mother can answer so well! She never tires of Maye's questions, like nurse; never says "don't bother" or "don't be tiresome." She knows so much of the birds and the flowers! and through the medium of the glories and beauties of nature she leads the little mind to the love and realization of the Great Creator of it all.

Maye thinks the drive only too short, for they are already at Widow Barton's door. She is anxious to go in, but mother thinks she may perhaps disturb poor Johnnie; so Mrs. Forrester goes in alone, leaving the child in the carriage, with old John holding the pony's head.

The cottage door is open, and Maye can see right into the inner room, where poor Johnnie is lying in bed.

His eyes are shut and his cheeks are flushed with fever. Maye sees Widow Barton look up gratefully at her mother when she comes in, and the poor woman's eyes are full of tears.

Then Maye sees mother bend over the sick boy, and feel his head and his hands. She takes off her hat, and gently lays her cool hand on his burning forehead, and Maye thinks how white it looks by his red, red face.

Then she gets a wet bandage, and lays it on his head gently and tenderly, every now and then looking up, to speak consolingly to the poor widow, who is crying by the bedside.

There is a little lattice window in the inner room, and the sun, streaming through it, gleams on mother's golden hair as she bends over the bed; and Maye thinks how like she looks to a picture in the gallery at home, of an angel who is leaning over a little dead boy, and preparing to fly with him up to heaven.

Bye and bye, it seems to Maye as if it really *were* that picture, and *not* mother, that she is looking at: for everything is getting indistinct:—the cottage, and the lattice, and the room, are fading away; and only mother and Johnnie getting more and more bright! Presently, they seem to move! Johnnie and mother, bending over him, are slowly moving, up, up, up, towards heaven!............

"Why Maye, my darling! fast asleep!"

Maye starts up, and finds the cottage is there, and the lattice is there, and Johnnie is there, and mother is standing by the pony-carriage with her own bright smile.

" Is it *really* you mother ?" says poor little Maye, " Oh, I am so glad !"

" Really me, darling ! why of course it is ! have you been dreaming, dear ? What was it all about ?"

But somehow Maye does not feel inclined to tell her mother her dream, and the recollection of it weighs on her spirits. She is not thoroughly herself again till they have driven some way on, and she finds her mother is really laughing and talking as usual.

They stop at the doctor's door, to tell him to go and see poor Johnnie, but the doctor is out; " Very busy indeed," his servant says, so they leave a message for him and drive home.

Leaving the pony-carriage in the stables, they cross the farm-yard behind the house, and go through the fields and the meadows to meet father.

And running about in the green grass with mother, gathering buttercups and the pretty wild flowers, every now and then pausing to listen for the hoofs of father's horse ; Maye soon forgets her troubles.

Gervase Forrester, riding home in the lovely spring afternoon, was listening to the song of the birds, and revelling in the sweet sounds, till there came borne to him across the fields, the soft voices and rippling laughter of his wife and child ; and then he cared no more for the warbling that had before so delighted him.

Then, when a turn of the road brought them in sight, he reined in his horse to watch them coming to meet him, and his eye drank in with love and pride the beauty of both :—the graceful form and light step of the golden-haired mother, the fairy form, and bounding step of the golden-haired child, with the green fields around them, and the cloudless sky above !

And when Maye was lifted up in front of father on his horse, and rode home with his arms around her, and mother walking by the side, all dreams and perplexities had vanished, and there was not a happier child in the county than little Maye Forrester.

But the pleasures of that birthday are not half over, for Maye is to have tea in the drawing-room. The drawing-room bread and butter is as different as possible to the nursery kind, and Mother pours out the tea quite differently to nurse.

"I wonder" reflects Maye, as with a sigh of deep satisfaction she seats herself at the tiny tea-table, and watches her mother actually putting *cream* into the pretty cup that is coming to her ; "I wonder why everything about mother, is so much prettier and nicer than anywhere else." Father drinks a cup of tea, "just to please Maye," but he seems to like it very much all the same. ✓

After tea, there are all sorts of games, "Puss in the Corner," and "Hunt the Slipper," and "Here we go round the Mulberry Bush ;" till Maye is quite tired out, and is glad to sit in the window on her father's knee while mother goes to the piano and sings " Little boy blue" and " Poor Cock Robin."

Bye and bye, the sun goes down and the soft evening twilight comes. " Sing us some song to suit this lovely evening,

Mabel," says her husband, "it must be something plaintive and touching, you know, almost melancholy, if you will."

Mabel Forrester did not answer for a minute ; then running her fingers lightly over the keys, she said, laughing softly "You have asked for a melancholy song, Gervase, and you shall have it. It is one I am very fond of myself; but I am not sure you and Maye will not think it a little too sad for a birthday evening."

She played a few chords, and began,

> "It may be God, who saw our careless life,
>   Not sinful, yet not blameless, my sweet wife,
>   (Since all we thought of in our youth's bright May
>   Was but the coming joy from day to day,)
>   Hath blotted out all joy to make us learn,
>   That this is not our home, and bid us turn,
>   From the enchanted earth, where much was given
>   To higher aims, and a forgotten heaven."

Maye, nestled in her father's arms by the window, feels an undefined melancholy creep over her, as she listens to her mother's song.

Mother's voice is so sweet and sad, and as it swells gently out, and mingles with the soft summer sounds in the garden, unbidden tears rise to the child's eyes, and the memory of her dream comes back to her.

Long will Maye remember that spring evening! Aye! golden-haired child ! never again will you hear the rustling of the breeze among the blossoms, the twittering of the birds, the note of the cuckoo, and the tinkle of the sheep-bell in the distance ; without blending with them the sweet sad tones of mother's voice, and the sweet sad words of mother's song.

"Hath blotted out all joy".........

All joy ! alas !

And when, half an hour after, Mrs. Forrester came into Maye's little bedroom, to hear her say her evening prayer ; she found the child in sobs and tears, and to all her enquiries and entreaties, she could get no answer but " oh mother I do love you so, I do love you so."

And she would not be soothed till she was taken in her mother's arms, and hushed and comforted as if she were still a little baby.

Then, as she lay with her golden head pillowed on her mother's breast, a calm came down on the little troubled soul ; gradually the sobs ceased, and she fell asleep :—and then her mother laid her gently back on her white pillows, and with a loving lingering kiss, left her to her innocent slumber, with the May moonlight streaming on her.

And so ended Maye's fourth birthday.

CHAPTER II

THE scarlet fever has broken out in the village,—said Gervase Forrester to his wife the next morning at breakfast.

Mrs. Forrester started, and the quick glance at Maye who was playing in a corner of the room, shewed where his first thought flew :—but before she had time to make any answer, her husband went on " I shall send you and Maye away if it spreads at all ; but there is no cause for alarm, as long as you keep clear of the village. It is a very bad form of scarlet fever, I am afraid, and has already been fatal in two cases."

" It is not near us at present, being chiefly on the other side of the mill. I fear, though, it is creeping round, for I hear Widow Barton's little boy................"

" What! Gervase " interrupted Mrs. Forrester, " you don't mean to say that little Johnnie Barton has this scarlet fever !"

Mr. Forrester was cutting some bread, and did not notice the expression of his wife's face.

" Indeed I do, dear" he replied " and I am sorry to say his is a very bad case, and the doctor gives very little hopes of his recovery. You see this black scarlet fever, as they call it, is so

C

very much more dangerous than the ordinary kind. I am very
thankful to think that poor little Johnnie and Maye have not
lately..................Good God, Mabel," he suddenly exclaimed,
dropping knife and bread in violent excitement as a sudden
recollection swept over him, " you went to enquire after him
yesterday! Don't tell me" he almost shouted, putting out his
hands as if to keep off what he dreaded to hear, " don't tell
me you went into the cottage !"

His wife's face answered him.

....

Maye, attracted by the clatter of the falling knife, looked up
from her game, and seeing something ailed both mother and
father, she ran towards them.

To her surprise and dismay, her mother recoiled from her,
and retreated to the other end of the room, dragging her father
after her.

" Gervase" she said hurriedly " Maye did not go into the
cottage ; we may keep her from infection if she is put at once
into strict quarantine : but she must go at once from me,
not come near me ; send her away, quick ! every moment
that she breathes the same air as me, exposes her to
danger ; only" she added in a lower tone " tell Nurse not
to frighten her about me, or to put any fancies into her
head—let her say I will meet her in the garden. She is
coming near me ; oh ! be quick, Gervase, send her up stairs.
Go away, child," she almost screamed, as Maye, more and more
puzzled, advanced towards her, " run up to nurse directly !"

Maye, bewildered and frightened, turned to go, but when she reached the door, she looked back to see if her mother was angry.

She saw her father take both his wife's hands in his, and say in a tone of forced calmness, " Now, Mabel, tell me exactly what happened. It may be we are alarming ourselves unnecessarily. It does not follow that because you went into the cottage you have exposed yourself to infection."

" Gervase, my own dear husband," said his wife earnestly, " do not deceive yourself. I held the boy in my very arms, I laid my hands on his head, nay, I even pressed my lips to his brow ; how *can* I escape ! Gervase, it is impossible !"

CHAPTER III

SADLY and wearily passed the June days to little Maye Forrester, and the child's mind was filled with perplexing doubts and fears.

For a change had come over everything.

She never saw her mother now;—never since that sad morning, when she had been so hastily sent from the Dining-room, had her eyes rested on her mother's face.

She was never allowed to go to her room in the morning, never allowed to go down to the dining-room breakfast, never allowed even to stray beyond the swing-door that divided the nursery wing from the other part of the house.

" What *could* it all mean ?"

" Could it be that she had been naughty ?"

The tender little conscience began to review the events of the last few days, but nothing presented itself to the innocent recollections.

" If she could only see mother just for a minute, it would all be set right she knew; but that was just the puzzle: they would *not let* her see mother, and *why*, oh why could it be ?"

Unfortunately, those early June days were very rainy, and so she could not go out; and she had been counting so much upon this, for Nurse had told her she might meet her mother in the garden.

Every morning she ran to the window, to see if it was going to be fine, and every morning the ceaseless down-pour met her disappointed gaze.

So the poor child roamed about the nursery, and listened to the pattering rain-drops against the window, and wondered what had happened to make everything so miserable.

She had asked Nurse many times why it all was, but that was *very* unsatisfactory. At first Nurse had said "wait till it gets fine, and then you shall go into the garden and meet her, and hear all about it"—but it never *had* got fine, and now, when she asked, Nurse (driven to her wit's end) had taken refuge in her old answers " don't bother," or " don't be tiresome," and Maye had once made up her mind that whenever Nurse said " don't bother" or " don't be tiresome," she would *never* ask her anything again !

And so the proud little heart shut itself up, and bore its misery as best it could—alone.

At last a day came when it seemed likely to be clear for a few hours, and Nurse had no peace till she had dressed Maye, and taken her out in the garden for the chance of meeting her mother.

The child's heart was light again, and she bounded along the terrace, singing and talking, keeping one eye on the door by which she thought it likely her mother would appear.

To beguile the time of waiting, it came into her head to gather her a nosegay " for a surprise."

This important work was begun at once, with all the solemnity due to so serious an undertaking.

First she tried to remember all the flowers that "mother loves best;" and this was no easy matter, for the memory at four years old is not very tenacious.

Then there arose a difficulty about reaching some of the flowers, and Maye was determined to have all the credit of making up the bouquet herself, so she would not ask Nurse's help, even though the stalks of the roses rubbed her little hands, and one hard-hearted thorn tried to make a hole in her poor little thumb.

The labour of love was completed at last, and with her hands full of flowers, and her cheeks flushed with her exertions, Maye ran joyfully up to Nurse.

" Look Nurse! *won't* mother be pleased !"

" Oh ! Miss Maye" objected Nurse, " the flowers are all wet with the rain, and look at your nice clean frock."

But her objections and reproaches were alike unheeded by Maye, for she had caught sight of her mother and father coming out of the house, and with one spring she was bounding towards them, when Nurse caught hold of her."

" Not too close, Miss, you must not go near."

Indignation lent Maye strength, and she broke from Nurse's grasp, and was rushing on, when to her astonishment and consternation, *Mother* herself called out to her to come no nearer ! .

It was too much for the impetuous tender-hearted child.

One moment she stood transfixed, as if she could not believe what she heard; and then in a passion of grief and wounded feeling, she turned and fled away.

On and on she ran, heedless of the voices that called to her to return ; on and on, out of the garden into the park, through the long avenue ; on and on, till she could run no longer ;—. and then, scattering far and wide the flowers she had gathered with so much love and care ; she stamped upon them with her little feet, till no trace of their beauty remained, and, flinging herself on the ground under an old beech tree, she gave way to such tears of bitter sorrow as had never before fallen from her eyes.

Many were the wild storms that had swept over that ancient beech tree, but never had it bent its lofty head beneath a wilder storm than that which now swept over the tiny child lying at its base. For the beech tree, rooted firmly in its mother earth, had had strength to withstand the fury of the blast; but the child's root in its mother's love had been shaken, and there was no foundation left to withstand the furious blast of wounded love and disappointment.

Mingled, too, with the grief, was a sense of injustice done ; and Heaven help the child whose faith in its mother's justice and truth has been taken away !

For this utter trust, this entire confidence, is the very essence of the purest, holiest love of which our hearts are capable ; in childhood we give it to our mother, in riper years we give it to our God.

To uproot this in a child, then, is to take away its religion, to throw down its altars;—the child has no mother, as the sceptic has no God.

When Maye was quite weary of crying, she got up from the ground, and then the reaction came. Her passion gave way to remorse.

There stole over her the conviction that it was her own naughty little self that had been unjust, and not the mother she loved so well; for it was a thoroughly honest little heart, and now that she was no longer blinded by passion, the child gave herself no quarter. Once more she seemed to hear the tones of the soft voice which had reached her ears even as she fled in her anger and passion, and to which she had not allowed herself to listen " Come back, Maye, come back, my darling, and hear what I have to say."

" Oh dear !" burst forth the child, wringing her little hands, " how could I be so naughty ! oh why did I not turn back. I wonder whether, if I run back quick, mother will still be there ! perhaps she is waiting for me, and wondering why I don't come."

At once she started off to find her way back, and to tell her mother how sorry she was she had been so naughty.

But, poor child ! she had not gone far before she met Nurse ; who had been looking for her everywhere, and who told her that her mother had got tired of waiting for her, and had gone home, that it was beginning to rain, and that she must come home too.

Maye's tears burst out afresh at this news, but she was to

miserable to resist, and so she walked home very quietly by Nurse's side.

But she cried herself to sleep that night when she found herself alone in her little white bed.

With the morning light came renewed hopes of a meeting in the garden, when she should by her docility and obedience, atone for her misconduct. But the day was rainy, hopelessly so ; the second day likewise : on the third Nurse told her that her mother was ill —was in bed ; and then the last hope was over, and the child gave way to despair.

She felt now in her remorse and sorrow, that if she might only tell her mother she was sorry she had not run back to her when she called, and feel her kiss of forgiveness ; she would be content to come back to the nursery, and enquire nothing more of the mystery that had clouded her happy little life.

Every day she heard that Mother was " no better" and " no better," and the remorse and longing grew stronger than ever.

Oh never tell me that childhood is the happiest time of life !

It may be that a child's sorrow is transient, but *while* it lasts I believe that it equals. if it does not surpass, ours in intensity.

There is something so hopeless, so unreasoning in children's grief.

They live so entirely in the present, that when the bright horizon is overclouded, it is with them the black darkness of hopelessness.

" All joy is darkened, the mirth of the land is gone."

D

So it seemed to little Maye Forrester through those dreary days, when the melancholy drip of the rain was only varied by Nurse and Letty's mysterious whispers.

At last there came a day when they talked and whispered more than ever.

All day long the rain pattered drearily on the window-pane, and the wind moaned and whistled all round the house.

It was a wretched day.

Maye did not care to play or talk, and was so peevish and miserable that Nurse, in despair, gave up trying to amuse or to please her.

She stood with her forehead pressed against the window-pane, looking out at the ceaseless rain, which was flooding the terrace, and spoiling all the pretty flowers.

In vain did Nurse try to coax her away: she was obstinate, and preferred standing there, gazing listlessly out; but she listened now and then to what Nurse and Letty were saying. "It can't last through the day" she heard Nurse say, and there followed a long whisper, mingled with deep-drawn sighs.

Bye and bye, they both went away, and the child was left alone.

So the afternoon wore on.

Towards twilight, Nurse came hurriedly back, and throwing herself into a chair, began to sob and cry.

Maye, standing with her little face to the window, would not so much as look round. She had made up her mind to ask Nurse no more questions; and restless and miserable as the child was, she felt half glad that Nurse had something to cry for too.

But the crying grew so violent that Maye at last looked round, and seeing Nurse rocking herself backwards and forwards in an agony of grief, the tender little heart was touched, and forgetting her pride, the child ran forward, saying, " Don't cry so, Nurse, what *is* the matter ? oh poor Nurse !"

" Oh dear, oh dear, Miss Maye" sobbed the woman "your poor mother's gone !"

" Gone !" echoed the bewildered child " mother *gone* ! where to, Nurse ?————

"Oh good Lord" cried Nurse " how am I ever to make the child understand—she is gone, Miss Maye dear, she's dead, poor dear lady !"

But the word conveyed no idea to the child's mind, and she only repeated " Gone ! mother gone ! without saying good-bye to Maye ! When is she coming back ? Nurse !"

" Heaven save us all" exclaimed Nurse " my poor child, the dead don't come back. She's never coming back any more Miss Maye—never any more !"

And Nurse hid her face in her hands, and her sobs and tears redoubled.

" Never coming back any more ! Mother never coming back any more ? Nurse !" exclaimed the child, bursting into a passion of tears, " you are very naughty, very wicked, to say such unkind things ; and I shan't listen to you, or love you a bit !"

" Letty" she added, turning imploringly to the nursery-maid, who now came in, "*you* won't say such bad things: it is'nt kind of Nurse, and it is'nt true, *is* it?"

"Answer me directly Letty" cried the child, stamping her little foot upon the ground, "why don't you speak?"

But Letty answered only by her tears.

The child looked from one weeping woman to the other, and her passion suddenly subsided. "Put me to bed, Nurse" she said wearily, and her arms dropped listlessly at her side, "I am very sleepy, very, very tired!"

An hour later, Nurse stole softly into the bedroom nursery, and seeing the golden head very still among the pillows, she was satisfied that the child had forgotten her troubles in sleep.

She returned to the day nursery, remarking to Letty "She did not understand, poor lamb! but we will let her sleep to-night, and to-morrow I will try to explain it better."

"She was dead tired, poor child" added Nurse, sighing, "and did not speak a word all the time I was undressing her. She must have dropped asleep directly."

But Nurse was mistaken.

Had she looked a little closer, she would have seen that the blue eyes were wide open.

The poor child had thought that if she could only get to bed, and to sleep, that she might wake as on a former occasion, and find it was all a dream.

But sleep was far from her.

Whichever way she turned, the words still rang in her ears "never coming back any more, never coming back any more."

She tried to shut them out by putting her hands over her ears, but she heard them all the same; even the " drip, drip" of the rain falling from the roof to the window-sill, seemed to sing the same sad song—

drip,

drip,

drip,

Never

coming

back

any

more.

" It is'nt true, it *can't* be true," sobbed the child in answer.

drip,

drip,

drip,

She's gone,

Miss Maye,

your poor

Mother's

gone.

" No, no, not without saying good-bye to Maye" urged the rebellious little heart.

drip,

drip,

drip,

Maye covered up her head, and hid her face, but still the

remorseless rain sang drearily on, and she could not get away from the sound, or help answering it.

Bye and bye Nurse came to bed, shading the light carefully from the child, lest she should disturb her supposed slumbers, and undressing quickly, she hastily extinguished the light.

Maye listened to Nurse settling herself in bed, and lay very quiet and still till the regular breathing proclaimed that she was asleep.

The moon now disengaged itself from the clouds, and sailed along the sky, surveying the damp earth beneath, and making the rain-drops on the trees and flowers glisten like so many diamonds.

It lit up the park, the garden, and the terrace; and then resting with a pitying eye on a little window in the left wing of the house, it flooded the bedroom nursery from one end to the other.

Then, when all was still, the golden head raised itself from the pillow, and noiselessly the child slid out of bed.

Stealthily, and on tip-toe, she crept to the door—then looked back at the sleeping form in the bed.

But Nurse did not move, and Maye opened the door.

It creaked loudly, and the child's heart leapt to her mouth.

Again she looked back at Nurse, but all was quiet; so gaining courage, she sped on into the next room, and by the light of the moonbeams found her way across it, and reached the passage.

Pitter-patter go the little bare feet along the passage, and pass through the swing-door into the corridor.

"MOTHER!" WAILS THE LITTLE VOICE "MOTHER! IT IS MAYE, ONLY MAYE,
OH DEAR MOTHER! LET ME IN."

On a sudden, a passing cloud obscures the moon, and all becomes dark!

Maye's little heart flutters painfully, her breath comes quick and short, and she has half a mind to go back. It is very cold, too, and she shivers in her little white nightdress.

She fancies she sees dark forms hovering round her, and every tale of horror she has ever heard, comes crowding thick and fast upon her brain.

How shall she *ever* cross the long dreary space that lies between her and Mother's room!

Shall she turn back?

But no! the longing for Mother is too strong in the infant breast; so pitter-patter she goes again along the corridor; and every step is bringing her nearer to Mother!

Pitter-patter, pitter-patter; at last the door is reached.

The child raises herself on tip-toe, and the little hands wander all over the door to find the handle; at last the trembling fingers reach it—turn it, but turn and turn in vain.

The door is locked!

"Mother!" wails the little voice "Mother! it is Maye, only Maye, oh dear Mother! let me in."

But no sound comes from the room, no voice replies; all is silence and darkness.

"Mother!" and the poor little voice rises to a sob, "I have something to say to you; oh Mother! let me come in!"

Still no answer; no sound but the moaning of the wind, and the echo of the child's lament.

Despair takes possession of the forlorn little heart; when suddenly a thought comes into the child's head.

She will go through the dressing-room!

The door is ajar, and softly the little shivering figure passes through, and reaches the door that communicates with the bedroom.

But now..............what if *that* door should be locked, too!

The handle is found—it turns—it yields—it opens!............ ....and the golden-haired child stands on the threshold of the fever-haunted room, from which by so much care and love she has been debarred!

Pitying angels are there none to stay the baby footsteps? to motion back the little white-robed figure ere it be too late?

The room is cold and chill, for all the windows are wide open, and it is dark, very dark.

The child stands in the doorway till her eyes grow accustomed to the obscurity, but by degrees she discerns the many familiar objects in the room; the table, the chairs, the curtains, the bed...........and yes! Maye can dimly see a form lying there, lying so still, so very still!——and with a cry of "Mother, Mother!" the child springs on the bed, and buries her golden head on that beloved shoulder.

"Dear, dear Mother" says the child "at last, at last I have found you! They told me you were gone away, and were not coming back any more, but I knew you would not go without saying good-bye to me. Why have you kept away from me all this time, Mother? oh why did you tell me not to come to you?"

But Mother does not answer.

"I have come in the cold and the dark, Mother, to find you; won't you just wake up one little bit to speak to me?................. ....I am so cold, Mother, so very cold........................ ....Mother, dear, if you are so very tired, I won't wake you up, but I will just tell you *very* softly all I have wanted to say for so long."

" Oh Mother ! I *wish* I had not run away that day, and I *wish* I had run back when you called me ! When you wake up and call me *again*, dear Mother, I will run close, close to you ; you won't tell me again not to come near, *will* you : and no one shall ever take you away from me any more................................ Do you hear what I am saying in your dreams, Mother ? ....oh how I wish you could just wake up for a minute to give me a kiss................................ And oh ! Mother ! why wouldn't they let me come and say my prayers to you ?"

"I haven't said them for a long while, I should think not for three years ! I wouldn't say them to Nurse. Was that *very* naughty, Mother ?"...................

"Let me say them now : might I say them lying down just for once, because I am afraid of waking you if I move, and you seem so tired, *so* tired, Mother !................................ ' Pray God bless Maye's dear Father and Mother, and '............ oh ! I am so cold................so cold, Mother !..............................

....

The moon, once more breaking out from behind the clouds,

shines through the open windows, and sheds a pale light on the dead Mother, and on the sleeping Child.

drip,

drip,

drip,

goes the rain upon the window-sill, but it is only answered now by the sighing and the moaning of the wind—

drip,

drip,

drip,

but its sad song is unheeded ; for sleep has overtaken the weary little child at last. The golden head is nestling close to the marble features, the soft round cheek contrasting with the pale hue of death.

The little hands are folded in the attitude of prayer, and a smile plays about the baby lips; as if in her dreams the forgiveness has been spoken, for which she has pined so long :— as if in her dreams has been vouchsafed to her the sense of that presence, and of that love, which she will in life enjoy, never, never again—never again !

Such was the sight that greeted the eyes of Gervase Forrester, when in the cold grey of early morning, he entered the chamber of death.

"THE MOON, ONCE MORE BREAKING OUT FROM BEHIND THE CLOUDS, SHINES THROUGH THE OPEN WINDOWS, AND SHEDS A PALE LIGHT ON THE DEAD MOTHER, AND ON THE SLEEPING CHILD."

CHAPTER IV

GREAT was the confusion that reigned at the Hall a few hours later.

The servants, with faces of consternation, ran some one way and some another.

Quarantine was forgotten in the general excitement, and all mingled freely together.

A horse was hastily saddled, and a man galloped madly off for the doctor.

In the servants hall a group was assembled, all questioning, answering, wondering, and crying at once.

But the upper housemaid had the most to tell, for she had actually met the widower coming out of the chamber of death, carrying the child in his arms.

"I was passing my poor dear lady's room" she proclaimed to her attentive audience, "before six this morning, when to my surprise, I saw the door was open. Knowing that Mr. Forrester had the key, I was rather startled, and was hesitating whether I would go in, when I heard a sound like a groan from within, and my master's voice saying "Both! must I lose both! oh my God this is too much!

"I had hardly time to step back, before the door was

violently pushed open, and he came out, carrying dear little Miss Maye, fast asleep, in his arms!

" To my dying day, I shall never forget his white ashy face, and set features!

" He didn't even see me, but strode on towards the nursery, calling to Nurse, and shouting for some one to go for the doctor.

" To think" concluded the housemaid, bursting into tears " that after all the pains my dear, dear lady, and everyone else, took, to keep the child from infection, that the innocent lamb herself should fly in the face of Providence in that way."

Many and various were the voices that broke in upon the close of the housemaid's speech.

Some now remembered having heard wailing and whispering in the dead of the night: others had heard, or fancied they heard, the pattering of footsteps along the corridor.

The under-housemaid deposed to hearing the passage-door swing, and Letty, the nursery-maid, to hearing the rattling of a door-handle.

" Why did I not get up?" sighed one " and see what the whispering was."

" I might have guessed" burst forth another "that the passage-door would not swing by itself."

" It was all my foolish fear of ghosts" sobbed a third " that prevented me running down to see who was walking about at that hour of the night."

" Now it is too late" chimed in the old butler " Miss Maye will have the fever, and our poor master will be................."

Here the door opened, and a groom, whose dusty dishevelled appearance testified to the speed with which he had ridden, informed the eager group that the doctor had arrived.

" The child is suffering from a severe chill, brought on by so many hours exposure to damp and cold in a thin night-dress.

" I fear there are already one or two rheumatic symptoms, so she will require the utmost care.

" That it will end in scarlet fever, I cannot attempt to disguise from you. Indeed it would be a miracle did she escape after so long a contamination."

Such was the verdict that fell from the lips of the doctor on the ears of Gervase Forrester, as they stood together by the child's bedside.

It was now some time since she had been put into a warm bed, and every means tried to infuse warmth into the numb'd little limbs.

Indeed, so cold had been every member of the poor little frame, when her father had found her, that for some minutes he had doubted whether she were not as lifeless as the Mother by whom she lay.

The doctor rose to take his departure, with kindly sympathetic words and manner. The Father was very calm, very quiet ; his voice did not falter as he thanked the doctor for his speedy answer to his summons, and accompanied him to the door.

But when he returned to the bedside of the still sleeping child, his face was white with suppressed emotion, and his features worked painfully with his efforts to hide his grief.

He stood gazing for a minute with an expression of yearning tenderness on the little face on the pillow; and then sitting down by the bedside, he buried his face in his hands.

A slight movement—the child turned uneasily in her bed, and an expression of pain passed over her face, as she tried to move.

She fixed her eyes with a look of perplexity on the bowed figure in the chair.

" Father, is that you ? where's Mother ?"

It might have been a voice from a sepulchre that answered " Gone, Maye, gone."

" You should not tell stories, Father," said the child gravely " you know quite well that Mother is in her bed, lying very quiet and still. Nurse told me she was gone, so I went last night to see. It was so cold and dark, Father, all the way ; oh ! so cold ! But I found her at last ! and she kissed me and held me tight, and said I should never go away from her any more !"

" But when I awoke, Father" continued Maye mournfully, and the light of excitement fading from her eyes " I found myself here in my own bed, with you sitting by. How did I come out of Mother's room, Father ? who brought me here ? ....how is it all ?............" and the child passed her hand wearily over her brow " oh Father ! my head aches and all my

bones ! *please* make me warm ! oh I feel as if I should never
be warm again."

Gervase Forrester bent over his little daughter, and summon-
ing Nurse, they did all they could to warm the cold limbs,
with hot applications.

Anxious also to subdue her excitement, he soothed her to
the best of his power without answering her questions ; and
the pain she was now suffering in all her joints put the
subject out of her head, and she began to cry.

Bye and bye she fell asleep, and slept at intervals for the
rest of the day.

The next few days she suffered greatly ; it was acute rheu-
matism in all the joints, and the doctor was very fearful of
the result should scarlet fever set in in a very severe form.
Gervase Forrester never left his child's bedside during those
days of pain and anxiety, till he was forced to tear himself
away for a few hours to attend the funeral of his fair young
wife.

The bright July day seemed a mockery to his feelings as he
entered the green churchyard, and stood by the open grave.

" Ashes to ashes, dust to dust."

The solemn words had been spoken, the bell had ceased to
toll, and the funeral train had departed ; but still Gervase
Forrester stood motionless, gazing down upon the narrow
space that contained all that remained to him of the fair young
companion of his youth.

Not a month ago, since, as he rode home, he had heard the

merry voices in the fields, and wondered as Mother and Child came to meet him, which was the fairest and the brightest!

Now where were they?

Hushed were the merry voices, dimmed were the laughing eyes: one struck down by the hand of death in the very zenith of youth and beauty, and of all that makes life a heaven upon earth;—and the other tossing about on a bed of pain and sickness, the fairy limbs contracted with agony, and the merry clatter exchanged for the restless moan.

He thought of the gentle mission of charity which had caused it all, and a strong feeling of resentment burnt in his breast as he thought of the Widow and her boy.

She might have known, have guessed, before she let in the Joy of his Manhood, the very Light and Brightness of his home, to her fever-haunted cottage!

In the excitement of his feelings, he for the first time raised his eyes from the ground, and they fell upon a little, open grave, close by.

A terrible presentiment came over him.

What could it mean!

Whose could it be!

He tried to shake off the superstitious feeling, but it would not go.

There, before his eyes, was his wife's open grave, and there by its side, ready-made, as it seemed, was a child's!

He made a step towards it; and then, half ashamed of his superstition, he turned abruptly and hastily round, and............ came face to face with Widow Barton.

The poor woman's eyes, suffused with tears, were raised timidly and pleadingly to his; but the very sight of her was too much for him in his present frame of mind, and he involuntarily recoiled from the author of so much woe.

"Oh Sir!" began the poor widow, but the words died on her lips as she saw the expression of his face.

Without a word or a look, he brushed past her, and with bitter feelings in his heart, he strode on through the church-yard.

Only, when he reached the little gate, he turned to take a farewell look at the grave ; and saw the poor woman make her way to the tiny new-made grave, and throw herself, disconsolate, beside it.

A light broke upon his mind.

It was *her* boy, then, who rested so close to his precious dead !

He, who had caused her death, should rest by her for ever ! —and with a mixture of bitterness, jealousy, and withal a sense of relief, in his heart, Gervase Forrester pursued his way to his desolate home.

All night long, and for many days and nights, did the Father listen to the ravings of his child.

The scarlet fever had set in.

Every feature of the disease recalled vividly to him the

F

death-bed he had so lately attended, and he was hopeless from the first.

Fearful indeed was it to witness the battle between the fever and the child; many times did the doctors despair, so impossible did it seem that so slight a frame should cope with so powerful an enemy, aggravated as it was by the child's weakness, consequent upon the previous attack of rheumatic fever.

Sometimes, in her wanderings, Maye would fancy herself stealing along the corridor and moan that it was dark, all dark: and that she should never find her way!

Then she would shriek out that horrid forms were round her, and guarding the door to her Mother's room.

Fixing her eyes upon her Father, she would implore him to defend her from them.

Or, she would think her long dark walk was over, and she was safe in her Mother's arms. Then she would become soothed and quiet, and imagine herself talking to the Mother, whom on earth she could never meet again.

These touchingly simple conversations would melt all present to tears, by the strength of her baby love they revealed, and send her Father rushing from the room.

But the fever was worsted at last, the crisis was safely passed —and pale, emaciated, with her golden hair cropped close, and the round beauty of childhood gone, little Maye Forrester was brought from the brink of the grave, and pronounced out of danger.

And then the giant, Fever, was satisfied, and stalked off to other places to continue its work of destruction; leaving behind it the homes it had blasted, the hearts it had lacerated and broken, and the new green graves in the churchyard !

CHAPTER V.

N the long hours of recovery, when the child was strong enough to bear it, Gervase Forrester laboured gently and gradually to make Maye understand that her Mother was indeed gone.

He was not altogether unsuccessful, though his first introduction of the subject was met with such a burst of tears and incredulity, as utterly appalled him.

By degrees, the idea of death and eternal happiness dawned indistinctly on the child's mind.

Not that it was the first mention of these things, for Mabel Forrester had early inculcated, as only Mothers can, the great, though simple, truths of religion.

But it was one thing for the baby understanding to accept these instructions in a general way :—and another to bring them home to the young Mother, who had so lately joined in all her childish pastimes, and glorified her happy little existence.

Still, by patience and perseverance, it was done at last. Every day, and little by little, it was gradually broken ; for the child was weak and fearfully excitable, and it could only be touched upon at times.

But as the time went on, Gervase Forrester discovered what puzzled him not a little as to the course to pursue, and that was Maye's firm belief that she had indeed been spoken to, caressed, and forgiven by her Mother, on that fatal night when she had lain for the last time by her side.

The child seemed to imagine that her Mother had died since; and Mr. Forrester saw that it was useless to attempt to argue on the subject.

He did not doubt in his own mind that Maye, falling asleep in the midst of her own confessions and enquiries, had dreamt that her Mother had really and actually responded to them; and he saw that if he removed the impression, he was taking away the child's greatest comfort and happiness.

So, after much thought, he decided to leave her the innocent delusion.

" Why" he argued to himself " should I dispossess the tender little heart of the recollection of her Mother's forgiving words and caresses ?"

" Why force upon her the cold hard truth that it was to the Dead she poured forth the wealth of her little heart's devotion ; and that the forgiveness she so pined for, did indeed remain unspoken to the last ?"

" No. I will let it be a treasure for the rest of our child's life ; a sweet memory of the Mother who will never be any-thing but a name henceforth."

These first difficulties overcome, there was much wherewith to comfort little Maye : many tender messages from the dying Mother were detailed by the Father with loving minuteness.

As Maye grew stronger, she now and then alluded, in her innocent childish way, to her own misery during the weeks that preceded her illness.

Attracted by some remark she made, her Father questioned her on the subject, and bit by bit he drew from her the recital of her sorrows.

It made his heart ache to hear the weak little voice detailing all the longings, perplexities, and regrets of those sad days ; more especially when he perceived that the mystery, over-shadowing all, had added tenfold to her unhappiness.

The story of the flowers touched him greatly, and he deeply regretted that this tender little attention of the child's should never have been known to his wife.

" If I had only guessed *why* it all was Father" said Maye, when she had finished the whole account, and had sunk back somewhat exhausted on the pillow " it would not have been *half* so bad. I don't understand it now, you know" she added wistfully, with a look in her eyes that said plainly she would demand an explanation if she dared.

The timid appealing glance was almost too much for the Father, whose whole soul was moved with pity and love by the tale he had now heard.

He took the little transparent hand in his, and tried to explain the danger of infection, and how that it was in love, and not in anger, that she had been kept away from them all.

He told her that they had purposely desired that nothing should be explained to her, lest she should take alarm at the thought of her Mother's probable illness.

That her Mother had always intended meeting her in the open air, and gently preparing her herself for what might possibly come ;—which intention had been frustrated first by the inclemency of the weather, and then by Maye herself.

Gervase Forrester was anxiously watching the little pale face as he proceeded with his explanation, and its expression warned him that he must not linger on this part.

He therefore hurried over it, and hastened to conclude.

He was not able to judge how far the heart of his little daughter was comforted by his words, for she had closed her eyes, and was lying very still ; but as soon as he had ceased speaking, she opened them and raised them to his, while a faint smile stole over her face. "Father" she whispered, squeezing his hand very tight in both of hers "I'm *so* glad you told me. I always thought you and Mother didn't love me any more, and I couldn't think why."

"I am only sorry now about the flowers; they were so beautiful, and just those Mother loved best. It was so naughty of me to stamp on them, and now" she added mournfully, "they are quite lost, and Mother will never, never get them."

"Can you remember their names, Maye," said her Father suddenly, after a pause of some minutes.

"Oh yes, Father" answered the child "for I have thought of them so often since I was naughty that I know each one by heart."

She repeated the names, and Mr. Forrester wrote them down in his pocket-book, and put it into his pocket.

" And now, darling" he said, stooping over the bed, and tenderly kissing the attenuated little face " you have talked enough, so I shall leave you for a little while. Go to sleep, and forget everything that ever made you unhappy.

" Only for the future, my child, try and remember that however dark and mysterious your Father's dealings with you are, there is some great, wise, and merciful purpose hidden beneath his seeming severity."

He must have been speaking more to himself than to the child ; for as he ended his simple warning, his voice faltered, and the concluding words were so inaudible that she did not hear them.

" God knows I need the lesson now myself !" he murmured as he drew down the blinds, and closed the shutters.

And then he broke down utterly, and hastily left the room.

" And so" said Maye to herself, with a sigh of relief, as she closed her eyes, and clasped her little hands tight together " and so neither Mother nor Father were angry with me after all !"

And sleep overtook her with a happy smile still playing about her parted lips.

CHAPTER VI

IT was a lovely evening in August, when two figures in deep mourning might have been seen at the gate of the little churchyard.

They were those of Gervase Forrester and his little daughter.

They were leaving for the Continent on the following day for two years, and Maye was come at her own urgent request, to visit her Mother's grave.

Threading their way among the many nameless hillocks, they reached a secluded corner, where, beneath a spreading yew-tree, the wife and mother lay sleeping.

Gervase Forrester looked anxiously at his child as they stood in silence before it, but the tightened clasp of the little hand that rested in his, was the only sign of emotion she showed.

There was a plain marble tablet at the head of the grave, and a railing enclosed a little garden, where blossomed some beautiful flowers.

The child's eyes, painfully large and lustrous from recent illness, wandered eagerly all over the grave, drinking in the minutest details.

G

Heaven knows what the child had expected to find there! or what vague hopes and dreams had filled her little mind as to her Mother's last resting-place; but certain it is that a shade of disappointment came over the little thin face as her eye glanced over the tablet and the mound—till it rested on the flowers.

And then the expression changed.

A flush mounted into the pale cheeks, and she looked up eagerly and enquiringly at her father.

For there bloomed in that garden each flower of which the nosegay she had once gathered for her Mother had been composed!

" They were not lost after all, you see, Maye" came in low tones, the father's answer to the child's unspoken question "the flowers her darling gathered with so much care and affection, have reached her at last!"

Presently Maye pointed to the inscription, and whispered " Please read it to me, Father."

Distrustful of himself, and half fearful of the effect it might have on the child, Gervase Forrester hesitated, but the earnest blue eyes would brook no denial, and he read—

TO THE MEMORY OF

MABEL,

THE WIFE OF GERVASE FORRESTER,

WHO DIED JUNE 12th, 1866, AGED 21.

> "It may be God, who saw our careless life,
> Not sinful, yet not blameless, my sweet wife,
> (Since all we thought of in our youth's bright May
> Was but the coming joy from day to day,)
> Hath blotted out all joy to bid us learn
> That this is not our home, and make us turn
> From the enchanted earth, where much was given
> To higher aims, and a forgotten Heaven."

Very different were the hurried faltering tones to the soft plaintive notes in which those words had last fallen on the child's ear, but she recognized them at once, and with a half-stifled sob, she sprang from her father's side towards the tombstone, and hid her gushing tears behind it.

But Mr. Forrester, carried away by the association evoked by the words of the song, did not observe the little girl.

That last evening, with its every detail, is around him now!

He is thinking of the slight girlish figure at the piano, with the evening sunlight on her golden hair.

He is listening to the merry baby ballads, sung for the amusement of the child on his knee.

Standing brightly out against the dark background of the last few weeks, comes the recollection of each word that was uttered; of each note that was sung; of each expression in the ever varying, ever beautiful face!

He is sitting once more by the open window, with Maye nestled in his arms.

He hears again the soft happy laugh, and gay rejoinder which followed his request for a melancholy song: and the soft summer sounds in the garden blending with the music of his wife's sweet voice.

He remembers the undefined sadness that came over him as the words of the song fell upon his ear, and how, looking down, he had seen his own feelings reflected in the tearful eyes of the child.

But the sweet face at the piano had never for a moment lost its wonted look of happy serenity, the sweet voice had never faltered, the calm eyes had not been dimmed by a single tear. No! for that " this is not our home" was a truth neither sad nor strange to the pure spirit of Mabel Forrester!

....

And as this thought passed through his mind, the soul of the widower was comforted.

He woke from his retrospect of the past, and advancing to the grave, he rested his arms on the railing which surrounded it. "It was a type, Mabel" he murmured, looking down upon the green sod, where little Maye's flowers were glowing under the rays of the setting sun " that evening was a type of what now is."

" You—singing so calmly, so happily; while your child and I

sat apart from you with an undefined feeling of sadness rising within us; all that was but a foreshadowing of to-day- for you, far on high in the realms of Eternal Bliss, are now joining the glad song of Cherubim and Seraphim; while your child and I, here below apart from you, are filled with aching sorrow and desolation."

" But God be praised" he added, raising his eyes to the blue sky above "for the sure and certain hope of your perfect happiness in that Fair Place, where disease and death can never enter, and sorrow and sighing can never come !"..............

The cool breath of the evening air on his forehead warned him that it was time for the child to go home, and for the first time he missed her from his side.

She had strayed on to Johnnie Barton's small grave, and was gazing intently at it. The sight of her standing there in recovered health, by the very grave he had once feared might be her own, brought a feeling of deep gratitude to his heart ; and he reproached himself for not having sufficiently considered God's mercy in sparing his little daughter to him.

The dangers of the terrible illness through which she had safely passed came home to him, as he marked their effects in the fragility of the little figure that now came towards him, and in the exceeding thinness of the little hand that came nestling into his.

" Father" said the little voice " there is a tiny *hill* out there that I think must be little Johnnie's. Will you come and read me what is written on it ? It is *very* short."

A little while before, and Gervase Forrester could not have acceded to his child's request, but his recent meditations had soothed and softened him ; and he allowed himself to be led to the grave of the innocent author of all his grief.

" Father" said the little voice again, just before they reached the grave " I should very much like you to take me to see Johnnie's Mother."

Mr. Forrester's quickly averted head shewed that he was not by any means prepared for such a request ; but he checked the hasty negative that rose to his lips, and, anxious to avoid a direct answer, he read the inscription—

JOHNNIE BARTON,
AGED 4 YEARS,
"THE ONLY SON OF HIS MOTHER, AND SHE WAS
A WIDOW."

" Now if I do that I would not, it is no more I that do it."

" Father" said the persevering little voice " I should very much *like*, you know, to say good-bye to Johnnie's Mother !"

" You shall, Maye" he answered, turning suddenly to her, and revealing a face from which all bitter and angry feelings had fled away, " it is too late and cold for you now ; but I promise you we will stop at the cottage, on our way to the station, to-morrow morning. You and I,. Maye" he added gravely " have a great deal to say to Widow Barton, which we might have said long ago."

He took the child by the hand, and led her away.

" Farewell, Mabel," he murmured as he opened the gate, and turned to take a last long look at his wife's grave " one victory over myself has already brought me nearer to you."

" Good-bye, Mother, dear, *dear*, Mother, good-bye !" breathed the tiny creature at his side, as she kissed her little hand in the same direction.

The last golden rays of the sinking sun shone like a glory around the white tombstone in the distance, and illumined the figures of father and daughter, as they lingered together, taking their mute farewell.

The golden ball of fire sank into his bed, as the click of the latch sounded on the still air ; and the two figures passed out of the light, and disappeared down the road.

And then the darkness came down on the little green church-yard ; and no sound broke the solemn stillness, save the soft whisper of the summer breezes : which, playing with the message they had caught from the lips of the child, bore it lightly to the grave of the Mother, and gave it into the keeping of the flowers that slumbered there !

The next morning, at an early hour, Mr. Forrester's travel-ling carriage drove rapidly through the village, and stopped at Widow Barton's door.

He alighted, and lifting out his little girl, he took her into the cottage, and shut the door behind him.

Ten minutes elapsed—the horses pawed the ground impatiently, the coachman looked anxiously at his watch, and more than one voice exclaimed " We shall certainly lose the train."

The excitement was at its height when the door opened, and Mr. Forrester and Maye appeared, followed by Widow Barton.

When he had put Maye into the carriage, he turned back to shake hands with the Widow, and said a few words to her in a low voice.

" Now drive on quickly" he said to the coachman, as he seated himself by Maye's side.

And the carriage was soon out of sight.

The Widow remained standing at the door, gazing down the road, long after the carriage had disappeared.

Her eyes and her heart were full, but she was soothed and comforted.

For, with Gervase Forrester's kind words still ringing in her ears, with little Maye's kisses still lingering about her lips, a feeling nearer akin to happiness than any she had known since her boy's death, had come down upon the soul of poor Widow Barton.

" God bless them" she exclaimed fervently, as she returned to her homely avocations.

THE END.

www.ingramcontent.com/pod-product-compliance
Lightning Source LLC
Chambersburg PA
CBHW020253290326
41930CB00039B/1257